LEARN the ORDER of MASS

CASSIE LONGHEM

THIS BOOK BELONGS TO:

_____

_____

COPYRIGHT © 2024 CASSIE LONGHEM.

MASS:

THE TIME WE REMEMBER THAT

DIED FOR US.

4 MAIN PARTS (RITES) OF MASS:

1. INTRODUCTORY

2. LITURGY OF THE WORD

3. LITURGY OF THE EUCHARIST

4. CONCLUDING

MASS STARTS ... NOW!

THE
INTRO
(INTRODUCTORY)
RITE

IN THE NAME OF...

THE FATHER

AND THE SON

AND THE HOLY SPIRIT.

THE
LITURGY
OF THE
WORD

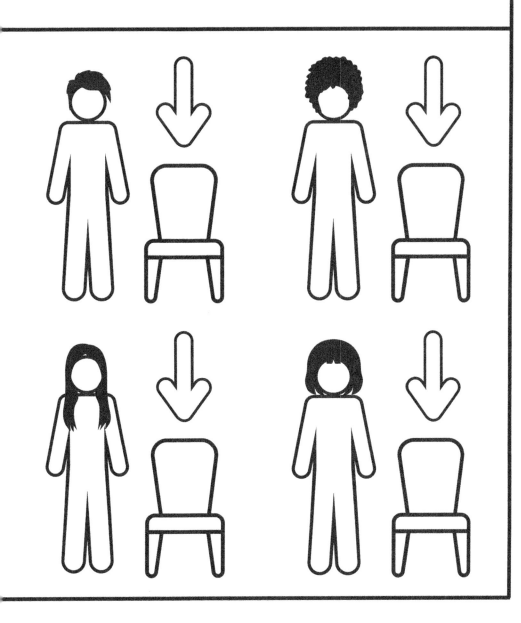

LISTEN to THE READINGS.

THE READER
(LECTOR)

READER SAYS:
"THE WORD OF THE LORD."

I SAY:
"THANKS BE TO GOD!"

PRIEST SAYS:
THE LORD BE WITH YOU.

EVERYONE SAYS:
AND WITH YOUR SPIRIT.

PRIEST SAYS:
A READING FROM THE HOLY GOSPEL ACCORDING TO (MATTHEW, MARK, LUKE OR JOHN).

EVERYONE SAYS:
GLORY TO YOU, O' LORD.

PRIEST GIVING the HOMILY

HOW DOES MY PRIEST LOOK? DRAW HIS FACE.

STAND FOR

THE CREED AND THE PRAYER OF THE FAITHFUL.

NICENO-CONSTANTINOPOLITAN CREED

I BELIEVE IN ONE GOD, THE FATHER
ALMIGHTY, MAKER OF HEAVEN AND EARTH,
OF ALL THINGS VISIBLE AND INVISIBLE.

I BELIEVE IN ONE LORD JESUS CHRIST, THE
ONLY BEGOTTEN SON OF GOD, BORN OF
THE FATHER BEFORE ALL AGES.
FOR US MEN AND FOR OUR SALVATION
HE CAME DOWN FROM HEAVEN,
(BOW FOR NEXT FOUR LINES)

AND BY THE HOLY SPIRIT WAS INCARNATE
OF THE VIRGIN MARY, AND BECAME MAN.
FOR OUR SAKE HE WAS CRUCIFIED UNDER PONTIUS
PILATE, HE SUFFERED DEATH AND WAS BURIED,
AND ROSE AGAIN ON THE THIRD DAY IN
ACCORDANCE WITH THE SCRIPTURES.

HE ASCENDED INTO HEAVEN AND IS SEATED AT THE RIGHT HAND OF THE FATHER. HE WILL COME AGAIN IN GLORY TO JUDGE THE LIVING AND THE DEAD AND HIS KINGDOM WILL HAVE NO END.

I BELIEVE IN THE HOLY SPIRIT, THE LORD, THE GIVER OF LIFE, WHO PROCEEDS FROM THE FATHER AND THE SON, WHO WITH THE FATHER AND THE SON IS ADORED AND GLORIFIED, WHO HAS SPOKEN THROUGH THE PROPHETS.

I BELIEVE IN ONE, HOLY, CATHOLIC AND APOSTOLIC CHURCH. I CONFESS ONE BAPTISM FOR THE FORGIVENESS OF SINS AND I LOOK FORWARD TO THE RESURRECTION OF THE DEAD AND THE LIFE OF THE WORLD TO COME.

THE
LITURGY
OF THE
EUCHARIST

SIT DOWN

FOR THE OFFERTORY.

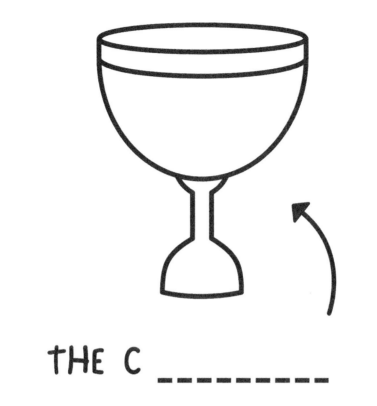

THE C _____

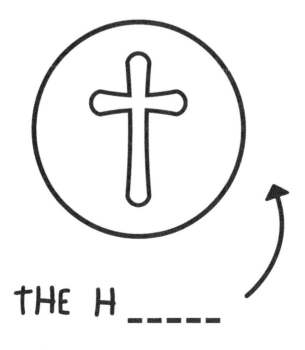

THE H _____

PRIEST WASHES HIS HANDS

WHY DOES THE PRIEST WASH HIS HANDS?

PRIEST SAYS HOLY, HOLY, HOLY (AND THE PREFACE ENDS).

KNEEL BEFORE

THE LAMB OF GOD.

 WHO IS THE LAMB OF GOD?

THE LORD'S PRAYER

OUR FATHER WHO ART IN HEAVEN HALLOWED BE THY NAME. THY KINGDOM COME, THY WILL BE DONE, ON EARTH AS IT IS IN HEAVEN. GIVE US THIS DAY OUR DAILY BREAD, AND FORGIVE US OUR TRESPASSES AS WE FORGIVE THOSE WHO TRESPASS AGAINST US. AND LEAD US NOT INTO TEMPTATION, BUT DELIVER US FROM EVIL. AMEN.

PRIEST SAYS:
JESUS WILL GIVE US
THE GIFT OF PEACE.

EVERYONE SAYS:
AMEN.

PRIEST SAYS:
THE PEACE OF THE LORD
BE WITH YOU ALWAYS.

EVERYONE SAYS:
AND ALSO
WITH YOU.

TELL YOUR NEIGHBOR
PEACE BE WITH YOU.

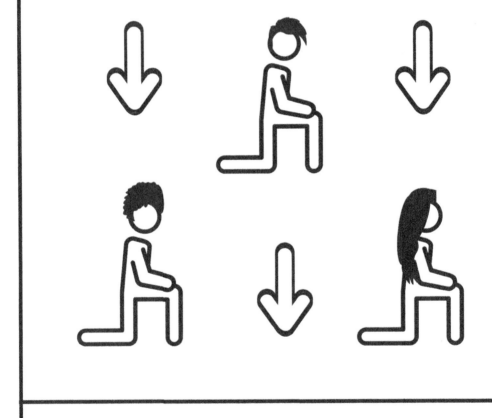

_____ OF CHRIST

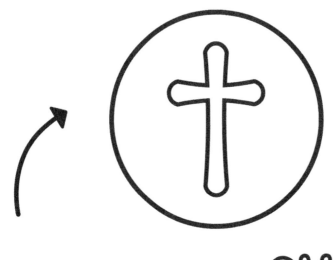

_____ OF CHRIST

THE CONCLUDING RITE

PRIEST SAYS:
"GO FORTH, THE MASS IS ENDED."

I SAY:
"THANKS BE TO GOD!"

END

OF

MASS.

MY DRAWINGS AND NOTES OF STUFF I SAW IN MASS

WEEK 2

Printed in Great Britain
by Amazon